DATE DUE		
AUG 19 2010	MAR 14 2013	
FEB 01 2011		
APR 22 2011		
SEP 12 2012		

Flying Machines

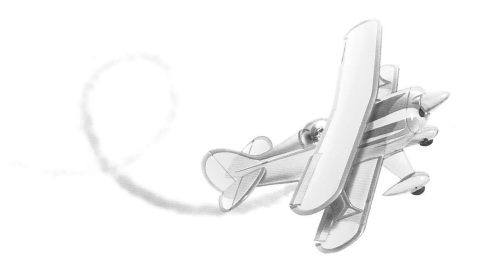

Angela Royston
Illustrated by
Sebastian Quigley

Heinemann Interactive Library
Des Plaines, Illinois

Contents

© 1998 Reed Educational & Professional Publishing
Published by Heinemann Interactive Library, an imprint of Reed Educational & Professional Publishing,
1350 East Touhy Avenue, Suite 240 West
Des Plaines, Illinois 60018

Library of Congress Cataloging-in-Publication Data
Royston, Angela.
    Flying machines/Angela Royston; illustrated by Sebastian Quigley.
        p. cm. — (Inside and out)
    Includes bibliographical references and index.
    ISBN 1-57572-175-9
    1. Airplanes — Juvenile literature. I. Quigley, Sebastian, ill.
II. Title. III. Series.
TL547.R683 1997   97-19350
387.7'3—dc21   CIP
                                                       AC

Photo credits: page 7, 11, 12 (centre right) and 18: © Austin J Brown;
page 8: Tony Stone Images © David Ximeno Tejada; page 12 (bottom left): © Britstock-IFA Ltd;
page 23 (top right): © US Air Force; page 23 (bottom right): © TRH/R Winslade.

Editor: Alyson Jones; Designer: Peter Clayman; Picture Researcher: Liz Eddison
Art Director: Cathy Tincknell; Production Controller: Lorraine Stebbing

Printed and bound in Italy.
See-through pages printed by SMIC, France.

02 01 00 99 98
10 9 8 7 6 5 4 3 2 1

Flying for Fun

Most flying machines carry passengers or cargo from place to place, but some people fly gliders and hang gliders just for fun. Gliders have no engines. They float gently on the wind.

Hang gliders are launched into the air from the top of a steep slope or cliff. The **pilots** steer by moving their bodies from side to side.

Gliders are towed into the
air by small planes. Then
they are left to fly like a
bird on the wind. Can you
see the pilot?

Passenger Planes

Big passenger planes carry people from one side of the world to the other. Jumbo jets are the biggest passenger planes. They have very powerful engines and need a long runway to take off.

On a long flight, a flight attendant brings food and drinks on a trolley. Would you like to watch a film during the flight?

Jumbo jets have huge wings. This one has four engines. How many wheels can you count?

This Concorde is coming in to land. It has swept-back wings and a pointed **nose**. It is the fastest passenger plane.

On the Ground

This plane has just landed. Workers move fast to get the plane ready for takeoff again. Trucks wait as the workers unload baggage, clean the plane, and load food for the next flight.

Air traffic controllers decide when aircraft can take off and land. They use computers and **radar** to make sure the planes do not fly too close together.

An engineer is lifted up so he can check the huge jet engines.

When the passengers have left the plane, the workers move in. Can you see the truck that pumps fuel from a storage tank under the ground?

Cargo Planes

Some planes carry things rather than people. The **nose** of this plane lifts up so that the load, called cargo, can be put inside. The cargo is packed into metal boxes called containers. Special trucks lift the containers up to the plane.

The inside of the cargo plane is a big, empty space. Can you see the rails on the floor? The containers slide along the rails on rollers.

10

The pilot then flies over the fire, and presses a switch to open the doors under the plane.

The water pours onto the burning trees. The plane flies back for more water.

Wheeling and Diving

I f you go to an air show you might see a team of planes doing flying stunts in the sky. Look how close together these planes are flying. Colored smoke streams from the engines as they wheel and dive.

This special plane flies upside down and can loop the loop.

This plane twists and turns to make a figure eight.

Even the best **pilots** have to practice for a long time before they can do these stunts.

In the Cockpit

The **cockpit** is where the **pilots** sit to fly the plane. Can you see all the controls and computer screens inside the cockpit? They tell the pilot about the plane's height, speed, and fuel.

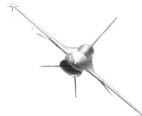

This screen shows whether the plane is flying level to the ground. The white line tilts as the plane turns. Can you see this screen in the cockpit?

The pilot of a warplane may have to get out fast. In an emergency, his ejection seat blasts out of the plane and **parachutes** to the ground.

There are two pilots in a passenger plane—the captain and the copilot.

The captain steers the plane with a **joystick** as it comes in to land on the runway.

Helicopters

A helicopter has long thin blades that spin around. They lift the helicopter into the air and move it up or down, forwards or backwards. Helicopters can **hover** in the air, and can land on a space as small as a rooftop.

Can you see the nets of supplies hung below this army helicopter? They will make loading and unloading quicker.

The **crew** of this helicopter watch for traffic jams in the streets below. They send reports to the radio station to warn drivers of delays.

Straight Up

Most planes need a long runway to take off, but jump jets can take off from a very small clearing. They can move straight up and down, like a helicopter.

Jump jets are painted special colors and covered with nets so they are hidden among the trees. How many can you see?

Each jet is flown by a **crew** of two. How do they get in and out of the jump jet?

Jump jets have grey **nozzles** that come from the engines. Can you see the nozzles on either side of the jet, just under the wings?

These nozzles can turn. When they point down, the jet lifts up into the air.

When the nozzles are turned to point backwards, the jet shoots forwards.

21

Warplanes

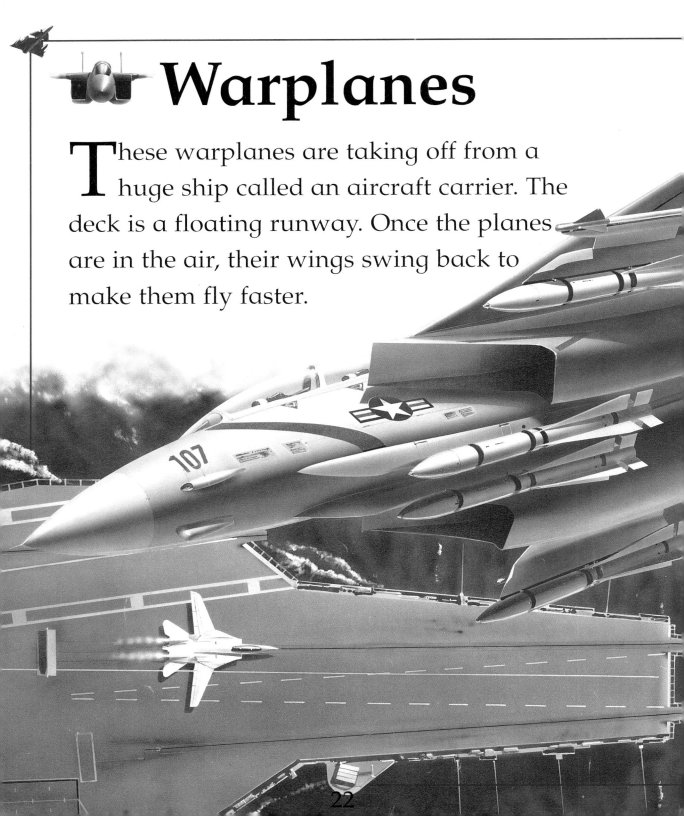

These warplanes are taking off from a huge ship called an aircraft carrier. The deck is a floating runway. Once the planes are in the air, their wings swing back to make them fly faster.

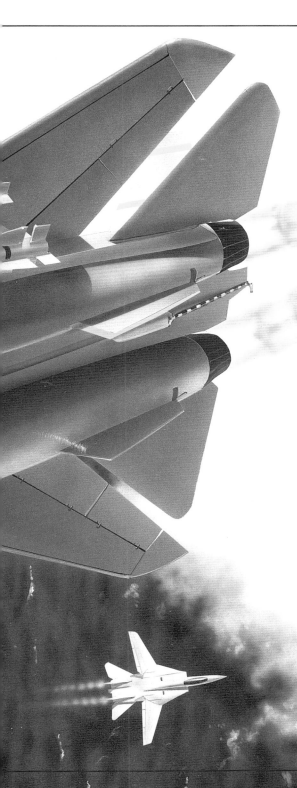

This strangely shaped warplane is called a Stealth bomber. It has been specially designed so it cannot be detected by **radar**.

This American fighter plane is over 50 years old. Can you see the **propeller** spinning round at the front?

Glossary

Cockpit   Part of a plane where the controls needed to fly it are.

Crew   Team of people who work together on a plane.

Hover   To stay in the air without moving.

Joystick   Lever used to steer a plane.

Military   Used by the army, air force or navy.

Nose   Pointed front of a plane.

Nozzle   Narrow opening at the end of a jet engine.

Parachute   Object made of silk that is used to slow a person down as they fall through the air.

Pilot   Person that flies a plane.

Propeller   Set of blades that spin round to move an aircraft forward.

Radar   Device that shows where in the air an aircraft is.

Runway   Long flat surface where aircraft take off and land.

Wheeling   Changing direction, turning.

More Books To Read

Otfinoske, Steven. *Taking Off: Airplanes Then and Now*. Tarrytown, NY: Benchmark, 1997.

Barton, Byron. *Airplanes*. New York: Harper & Row, 1986.

Mott, Evelyn. *Balloon Ride*. New York: Walker, 1991.

Index